SIMPLE PLEASURES

Candles

CONARI PRESS

First published in 2004 by Conari Press,
an imprint of Red Wheel/Weiser, LLC
York Beach, ME
With offices at:
368 Congress Street
Boston, MA 02210
www.redwheelweiser.com

Adapted from the *Simple Pleasures* series by Susannah Seton first published in 1996
by Conari Press.

ISBN 1-57324-960-2

Printed in the United States
PC

11 10 09 08 07 06 05 04
 8 7 6 5 4 3 2 1

The paper used in this publication meets the minimum requirements of the American
National Standard for Information Sciences—Permanence of Paper for Printed Library
Materials Z39.48-1992 (R1997).

Candle Magic

We are not sent into this world to do anything
into which we cannot put our hearts.
—John Ruskin

An easy way to make the house cozy is to use a lot of candles—in the bedroom, living room, dining room, even in the bathroom. They give a nice glow to a dark evening and, if scented, also add a soothing fragrance. Try anointing your candles with a few drops of your favorite essential oil—rose, bayberry, and vanilla are nice—or use your favorite combination for a customized scented candle.

You can also decorate candles with herbs and ribbons. Use large, slow-burning candles and attach small sprigs or herbs by using a richly colored ribbon. Be sure to always place candles on fireproof saucers, and never leave them unattended.

Simple Pleasures of Candles offers many more easy and affordable ways to decorate your house and garden area with candles. Also terrific housewarming gifts, these can be made in groups or while you're finding some quiet time for yourself. After you're done creating a Zen Centerpiece (page 54) or a Stained-Glass Votive (page 40), soak in one of the bathtub recipes offered here. But don't forget the main ingredient of any bathing experience— an array of candles to illuminate the room.

I love to bathe solely by candlelight. The warm glow gives a relaxing atmosphere to dream and let stress melt away. I used to live in an apartment with a nice-sized bathroom shelf that accommodated a dozen votives, but recently I moved and there seemed to be no suitable place for my candles. I thought I would have to give up this pleasure, but then I put up corner bracket shelves and mounted candle lanterns on them. Now, even when the candles are not lit, my bathroom has a wonderful exotic flair that everyone comments on!

5

FLOATING CANDLES

*C*andles do add a magical element to any room. I especially love the floating ones as a centerpiece for the dining room table. It solves the problem of having an arrangement that interferes with conversation. Simply float a few candles and some flowers in a bowl and you have an elegant focal point.

12 ounces paraffin
60 drops of your favorite essential oil
12 metal pastry tins or candle molds
12 1-inch floating candle wicks (available at craft
stores)

In a double boiler, melt the paraffin and then add the essential oil with a wooden spoon. Pour wax into molds slowly to avoid air bubbles. Let set partly and then insert wicks in the center of each. Let candles set fully and then unmold. Makes 1 dozen.

RESTORATIVE BATH

This bath a great pick-me-up.

cotton bath bag or piece of cheesecloth
2 tablespoons grated fresh ginger
1 ounce fresh rosemary
20 drops rosemary oil
20 drops lavender oil
1 cup rose water

Place the fresh ginger and rosemary in a cotton bath bag, or bundle in a 1-foot square piece of unused cheesecloth. Tie it closed. Place the bag under the bathtub spigot and run under hot water. Add oils and rose water to the bathtub, swirling with your hand to combine. The bath bag makes an excellent scrubber and exfoliator, and the ginger and rosemary will leave skin pleasantly tingling and feeling revived.

Light your favorite scented candles. Linger for awhile and let yourself relax and revive all at once.

CANDLES

PAPER CUP LIGHTS

These are great strung on your front porch or out on a deck for a party. The trick is to poke enough of the design in the cup to let the light through, but not to cut it completely.

cut-out patterns
solid colored paper cups
pencil
craft knife
large craft pin (looks like the letter T) or large safety
  pin
string of small indoor/outdoor Christmas lights

Find in a craft-pattern book or draw your own, a small design that will fit on a paper cup. (A small flower or a star works fine). Cut out the design to make a pattern. Hold the pattern against a cup you have turned upside down, and trace the design lightly onto the side.

With the craft knife, cut along sections of the pencil marks and push the cup in a bit along the cut. Do not cut out the design! The little cuts along the pattern will let the light through. With the pin, poke holes along the top and bottom of the design for effect. Punch a hole in the bottom of each cup the size of the Christmas lights and push the bulb through. String up when finished.

SAND CANDLES

These are some of the easiest candles to make yourself. They are great for outdoor barbecues—they actually repel insects—and they look beautiful too—as they burn more and more, the light shines through the sand. As with all candlemaking, be aware that wax heated too high can burst into flames. If this happens, turn off the heat and smother with a lid or damp cloth—do not pour water on; that will make it burn more!

damp sand (not too wet, about 1 cup water per bucket
  of sand)
large mixing bowl
smaller bowl, the desired size of candle
wick
paraffin
wax dye if desired

few drops citronella oil
candy thermometer
wicking needle

Pour sand into the large bowl until it's half-full. Tamp down with your fist. Push the smaller bowl into the sand and add sand around to fill in edges. Remove the smaller bowl, being careful not to disturb the remaining hole.

Measure the depth of the hole and cut the wick to fit, plus 1 inch extra. Heat the wax gently in a saucepan, adding the dye if desired and the citronella; mix well when the wax is melted. When the wax reaches 261° F, remove from heat and gently pour a bit into the center of the mold, trickling it over the back of a metal spoon so that the sand doesn't lose its shape. Wait about 5 minutes, as it seeps into the sand. Then add more, making sure the wax is still 261° F.

After about 2 hours, a depression will form in the middle of the mold. Again, heat the wax to 261° F and fill the depression. Push the wicking needle through the center of the well and lower the wick into the hole. Wind the top of the wick around the needle, and place the needle across the sand (so the wick stands upright).

In about 3 hours, the wax will have hardened completely. Remove the candle from the mold. Trim the wick and smooth the base of the candle with an iron on medium heat. Makes 1.

*I*f you want great sex, think about creating a bedroom that's conducive to intimacy, says Will Ross in *The Wonderful Little Sex Book*. "It doesn't need to be elaborately furnished, but it should be uncluttered, have pleasing colors, and not be merely utilitarian; it should inspire a sense of beauty. The bed you use for sex ought to have a special, exotic, otherworldly feeling, almost evocative of an altar. There should be an air of reverence. Some people enjoy making love under a canopy, and you may want to construct one. Soft lighting is immensely helpful [light several aromatic candles all over the room!], and so is quietly pulsating music. When the whole room feels like a retreat from the hustle and bustle of everyday life, won't you relish the thought of spending time there with your beloved?"

15

CANDLES

This bath feels luxurious beyond belief.

2 drops cedar essential oil
2 drops clary sage essential oil
2 drops lavender essential oil
2 drops orange essential oil
2 tablespoons vegetable oil

Combine all oils and pour the mixture into the stream of a warm bath. Before stepping into the tub, light tea lights on every surface in the bathroom.

*S*urprise your sweetheart with a candlelit dinner for two with your own home-made scented candles gracing both the table and the bed-room. Their lovely fragrance will be released as they burn. Scented candles are incredibly easy to make—you just need to plan in advance. (If you haven't planned ahead, you can still get some of the effect by sprinkling a drop or two of your favorite essential oil in the melted wax of a plain candle as it burns.)

2 ounces of your favorite fragrance essential oil (or try
   a combination; vanilla and rose are my favorites for
   romance)
¼ cup orris root powder (available at herbal stores)
1 large airtight plastic container big enough to fit 6
   candles
6 unscented candles, any size

Combine the oil(s) and the orris root and sprinkle in the bottom of
the container. Place candles inside, cover, and store in a cool spot for
4 to 6 weeks.

Candles are wonderful, especially as the dark creeps in earlier and earlier. If you would like to be intentional about the candles you use, consider the symbolism of various colors:

WHITE: spiritual truth and household purification

GREEN: healing, prosperity, and luck

RED: physical health and vigor

YELLOW: charm and confidence

CALMING BATH

The sensual delight of taking a bath in aromatic oils goes back to the Romans, who raised bathing to a high art. The public baths consisted of three parts: first you went to the unctuarium, where you were anointed in oils. Then you proceeded to the frigidarium, where you took a cold bath, then to the tepidarium for a tepid one. You finished with a hot bath in the caldarium. While we don't bathe as the Romans did, we can indulge in the essence of the practice.

4 drops bergamot essential oil
4 drops lavender essential oil
2 drops clary sage essential oil

Run a warm bath. Drop the essential oils into the stream of water. Slide in, and relax for 10 to 15 minutes.

CANDLE POTS

*O*ne of the easiest and most attractive arrangements you can make for a table or sideboard is a series of cream or white pillar candles in terra-cotta pots. Just group them attractively, and you have a simple yet sophisticated feeling. Make sure you never leave candles unattended; the moss can catch on fire if the candle burns too far down.

Dry floral foam
1 terra-cotta pot
1 pillar candle
glue gun
green, sphagnum, or reindeer moss
floral or straight pins

Trim the foam to approximately the same shape as the pot, making sure it is a little larger than the pot's diameter. Push the foam firmly into the pot until it touches the bottom. Trim if needed to get a good fit. Pack the spaces around the foam with moss. Trim top of foam level with pot. Glue candle to foam. Surround base of candle with moss, fixing it in place with pins. Makes 1.

HOMEMADE BUBBLE BATH

Bubble bath is a great gift that even small kids can make. The trick is to have a pretty container to put it in and to never divulge your ingredients.

> 2 cups Ivory (or other unscented) dishwashing liquid
> ⅛ ounce of your favorite essential oil (vanilla is my favorite)

Drop the oil into the dishwashing liquid and let sit, covered for 1 week. Pour it into beautiful a bottle and add a gift tag and ribbon and instructions to use ¼ cup per bath. Enough for 8 baths.

*M*ost hobby and craft stores carry everything you need to make candles of all sorts. But if you have trouble finding what you need, contact Cierra Candles (800-281-4337). Other good sources are Candlechem Co. in Massachusetts (508-586-1880), Pourette Manufacturing in Seattle (800-888-9425), and Longwyck Candle Works in New Jersey (800-724-8345).

Ten thousand flowers in spring, the moon in autumn, a cool breeze in summer, snow in winter. If your mind isn't clouded by unnecessary things, this is the best season of your life.

—Wu-men

HOMEMADE CANDLES

If you want to make your own candles, catalogues such as Hearthsong (800-432-6314) have kits. Or you can try the old standard we used to make in grade school. It's easy, but be careful—paraffin must be heated over low heat or it can explode. Never put it directly on the stove—only over a water bath.

block of paraffin (to equal 1 quart)
crayon bits for coloring
1 half-gallon coffee can
1 wick
1 pencil or chopstick
1 quart waxed cardboard milk or juice container,
    washed and with top cut off

Put the paraffin and crayon bits in the coffee can and place the can in a pan of water on the stove to create a double boiler. Melt the paraffin over low heat. Be sure to keep it over a very low flame, because paraffin explodes easily when overheated. While wax is melting, tie wick onto pencil or chopstick and place in the cardboard so that the pencil keeps the wick upright. When wax is melted, pour carefully into the milk or juice container and allow to harden completely overnight. Cut away container. Makes one pillar candle.

PINE BATH OIL

This oil is a great skin softener. Just pour a bit into your bath under the running water.

1 cluster pine needles
1 cup baby oil, approximately

Put the pine needles in a glass container with a lid. Cover completely with baby oil and cover tightly. Store in dry, cool place for 4 weeks. Strain the oil, and decant into attractive glass bottle. If you'd like, you can add fresh pine needles for decoration. Makes 1 cup.

Before slipping into this tub, light a few pine-scented and vanilla-scented candles to enhance your tub time.

The human body is the best
picture of the human soul.
—Ludwig Wittgenstein

FLOWERPOT CANDLES

Nothing can be easier than turning your old flowerpots into beautiful candle holders—wonderful for you and as holiday gifts. This is a Christmas holiday scent, but feel free to substitute your own favorite essential oils. This recipe is for one candle, but can be multiplied for more.

1 3-inch clay flowerpot
small piece of self-hardening clay
1 6-inch candle wick
1 small stick at least 5 inches long
1 ounce beeswax
1 ounce paraffin wax
15 drops cinnamon essential oil
15 drops mandarin orange essential oil

Plug the hole in the bottom of the pot with the clay and let harden. Attach one end of the wick to the stick. Lay the stick on top of the pot with the wick hanging down in the center of the pot.

In a double boiler, melt the beeswax and add paraffin. When melted, remove from heat and let cool slightly. Add the essential oils and mix thoroughly.

Pour the wax slowly into the pot, reserving a little bit. Fill to within ¼ inch of top. If a hollow forms around the wick as the wax cools, pour more wax into hollow. Once wax has hardened, remove stick by trimming the wick. Makes one candle.

CANDLES

*H*ot tubs can be expensive and time consuming. If you like the idea of bathing outside, consider buying an old-fashioned claw-foot tub (they cost about $100 and fit two people) for outside and run hot and cold water from the house out to it. Because you fill and drain the tub each time (let water trickle into your garden rather than wasting it), you're spared the hassle and expense of chemicals.

SKIN-SOOTHER BATH

This wonderful recipe will soothe any skin condition, from heat rash to chicken pox. It's wonderful for your skin and hair, so use it even you're your skin feels fine!

½ cup finely ground oatmeal
1 cup virgin olive oil
2 cups aloe vera gel
20 drops rosemary or lavender oil

Combine the ingredients in a large bowl; stir well. Add the mixture to a warm, running bath.

CANDLES

"STAINED GLASS" VOTIVES

Here's an activity my kids did in first and second grade that really turned out well and is worth sharing.

> small baby food jars
> tissue paper, different colors
> liquid starch
> ribbon
> tea light candles

Take small baby food jars, wash them thoroughly, and take off the labels. Cut different colors of tissue paper into small squares. Pour liquid starch in a spray bottle; spray starch on a jar and then apply squares of tissue paper all over the outside of the jar until completely covered. Let dry. Tie a ribbon around the neck of the jar, and place a tea light candle inside. When the light shines through, it is quite lovely.

*I finally figured out the only
reason to be alive is to enjoy it.*
—Rita Mae Brown

*A*s the weather begins to warm and you no longer use the fireplace, evoke the romance and beauty of a fire by placing four or five pillar candles inside it. The soft light they give off will compensate for the loss of the roaring fire.

43

FRAYED-NERVES BATH

7 drops lavender essential oil
2 drops sweet marjoram essential oil
3 drops ylang-ylang essential oil

Fill tub with warm water, and then add oils. Swish the oils around in the water to evenly disperse them, then submerge yourself.

*Y*ou can create an altar or other meaningful contemplative space in just about any nook or cranny of your house—a bookshelf, a ledge above the bathtub, a small table in your bedroom. The point is to pick a place where you will often go so that you can enjoy it. What you decide to place there is, of course, entirely up to you. But whatever you decide on should be something that has meaning for you. It should not be placed on your altar to please your Great-aunt Tilly who gave you that hideous green statue that you really wish some child would conveniently break.

DINING AL FRESCO

*F*or the past twenty years, I've lived in Southern California, and what I like best about it, besides no snow, is the opportunity it gives me to eat outside. We have a big picnic table and for almost three-quarters of the year we can have breakfast, lunch, and dinner outside. I love looking at my garden, smelling the air, hearing the birds, and feeling the sun on my skin as I eat. In the summer, we often host large dinner parties outside. I throw a few candles in old bottles of varying heights, and the side yard is transformed into a romantic courtyard. Even when it is too cold for three meals a day in the winter, whenever it is not raining I take my lunch out to the chaise lounge I've positioned in just the right spot to catch the weak winter rays, and enjoy dining out.

Here's an easy way to decorate your backyard for a sum-
mertime evening get-together—or just for yourself.

> silk flowers
> 1 strand of small white indoor/outdoor
>   Christmas lights
> ½-inch wide white or gold ribbon
> plastic or silk green leaves
> hot-glue gun

Pull apart the silk flowers and discard the stems. Take the
light strand and push a light through the center of a flower.
Continue until all lights are decorated with flowers. Hot-
glue the ribbon to an end of the light strand and begin
wrapping the cord. As you wrap, hot-glue the leaf stems
to the cord and cover the leaf stems with the ribbon.

FACIAL SAUNA

2 drops fennel essential oil
2 drops lavender essential oil
2 drops lemon essential oil
2 drops orange essential oil

Mix oils together and pour into a bowl of steaming water. Drape a towel over your head and the bowl and sit, allowing the steam to penetrate your pores. Be careful not to put your face too close—this should be luxurious, not a painful experience!

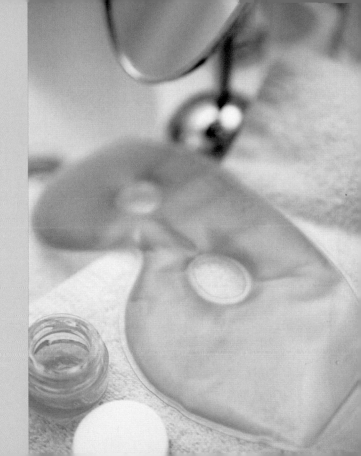

CANDLES

ZEN CENTERPIECE

Truly nothing could be easier than this arrangement; it will foster serenity wherever you place it.

small dark rocks
shallow bowl
3 small floating candles
1 flower such as a gardenia, rose, or hibiscus

Place the rocks in a colander and rinse. Fill the bottom of the bowl with 1 to 2 inches of rocks, depending on the depth of the container—you want to create a rock bottom. Fill with water up to 1 inch from the top rim. Float the candles and gently place the blossom on the water and allow it to float.

Every flower about a house certifies to the refinement of somebody. Every vine climbing and blossoming tells of love and joy.
—Robert Ingersoll

SIMPLE PLEASURES

Here's a great bath recipe for the winter, when skin gets so dry.

1 cup buttermilk
3 tablespoons Epsom salts
½ tablespoon canola oil
soothing essential oil of your choice, such as lavender
  or chamomile

Combine ingredients and pour into the stream of warm water as the tub is filling. Immerse yourself and relax for ten to fifteen minutes. Use the essential oil of your choice and scent and light a few large candles around your tub.

57

LAVENDER BATH OIL

Here's another great way to relax.

> 1 cup almond or grapeseed oil
> ½ teaspoon lavender essential oil
> ¼ teaspoon vitamin E oil
> dried lavender sprigs
> 10 ounce decorative bottle with a top
> ribbon and gift tag, if desired

Combine the oils in a glass container and test the scent on your skin. (You might want to add a bit more of one thing or another depending on the fragrance). Place the lavender sprigs into the bottle. Using a funnel, pour the oil into the bottle and close the top. Store in cool, dry place. Light a single lilac-scented candle and soak in your relaxing lavender concoction until your bath water completely cools.

CANDLES

CANDLE COLLARS

*A*nother wonderful way to dress up pillar candles is to make a candle collar. The candle must be fat enough to be safe and, again, you should never leave it unattended. To avoid accidents, make sure you place the candle on a dish so that the hot wax won't spread all over and snuff out the candle when there is an inch left at the bottom of the collar.

bay leaves, magnolia, or other
  attractive oval-shaped leaves
hot-glue gun
pillar candle
raffia

Put a little hot glue on the back of each
leaf near the base and press firmly to the
candle. Trim the bottom of the leaves so
that the candle stands evenly.

Tie raffia in a bow around the leaves and
the candle. Makes 1 candle.

CANDLES

POTTED CANDLE

bendable dry floral foam
6-inch terra-cotta pot
4-inch diameter candle
floral wire
solidago
lavender
larskspur
miniature roses
moss

Take the floral foam and cut a piece to fit inside the pot with about 3 inches of foam above the rim. Cut off the top 4 corners at a 45° angle. Push the foam down into the pot and then push the candle into the foam.

Make 8 small bunches each of solidago and lavender, and wire each bunch with floral wire. Beginning with the solidago, push the

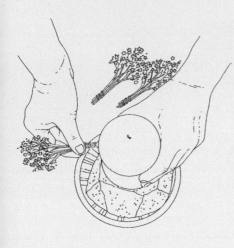

bunches into the foam on opposite sides to maintain a balance. The lavender bunches go in next in the spaces between the solidago. Move higher and lower as you go to create a thick ring of material.

Make several small, shorter bunches each of larkspur and roses and add them randomly, filling all small gaps. Rotate the pot as you work to notice how the flowers look from different angles.

When you are satisfied with the arrangement of the flowers, take some moss and place it around the base of the candle to cover the foam.